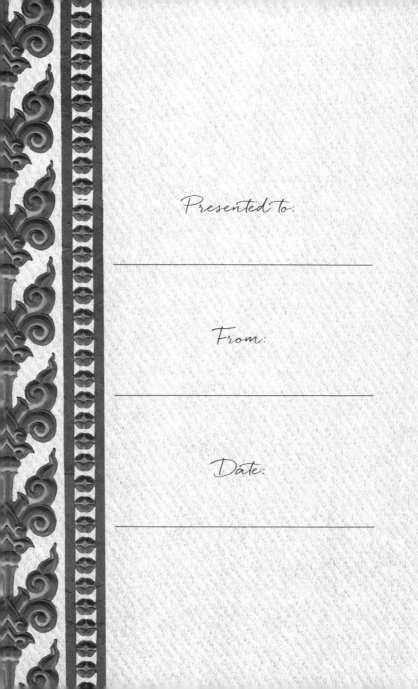

Presented to:

_____

From:

_____

Date:

_____

The God Who
Provides

100 Bible Verses
for Financial Wisdom

ZONDERVAN®

1

I [wisdom] traverse the
way of righteousness,
in the midst of the
paths of justice,
that I may cause those who
love me to inherit wealth,
that I may fill their treasuries.

PROVERBS 8:20–21

The Bible speaks of both wise and foolish living, but the way of wisdom and foolishness are separate paths that wind up in dramatically different places. Foolish living is easy, but wise living calls for intentionality on our part. The Scriptures warn, "Look carefully then how you walk, not as unwise but as wise" (Ephesians 5:15 ESV). No one has ever become financially stable by foolish living, but those who love wisdom are more prone to have wealth (Proverbs 8:21). Foolish living always says yes to every whim and desire. Fools live only for today and never plan for the future. When we walk in wisdom, we develop good habits that promote financial responsibility. Wisdom teaches us to exert self-control in the present so that we can meet our goals in the future. That means telling ourselves "no" or "not right now" when we need to so that we can stay on track and find greater enjoyment in meeting our long-term goals.

Father, thank You for Your many words on living wisely. Help me to guard against foolish living and to walk in wisdom. Please give me self-control and the ability to say no to myself when I should.

2

Wealth gained by dishonesty
will be diminished,
but he who gathers by
labor will increase.

PROVERBS 13:11

There is a famous adage that goes something like, "Opportunity is missed by most people because it is dressed in overalls and looks like work." Many people have tried to get rich by starting Ponzi schemes or luring others into scams. The Bible warns against such tactics. The book of Proverbs makes it clear that money obtained by fraud won't last, but those who do honest work will make their money grow (13:11). People who attempt to take shortcuts in life wind up getting nowhere or even falling behind. There is no shortcut to success. Financial stability requires making good choices over a prolonged period of time. Those who attempt to acquire wealth quickly by dishonest means will end up sorely disappointed. Success in any area of life calls for total commitment and a lifestyle of working hard. People with a good work ethic who make wise choices with money find that their efforts pay off, but those who are dishonest with money will end up worse than they started.

> *Father, please guide me as I strive to always be honest in all areas of my finances and to have an excellent work ethic. Help me to make good choices with my income.*

3

"Don't worry about tomorrow, for tomorrow will bring its own worries. Today's trouble is enough for today."

MATTHEW 6:34 NLT

God is faithful to provide everything we need to meet our daily challenges, but He distributes provision as we need it, and seldom in advance. Often we worry about things that never happen. Other times we worry about problems we will face weeks, months, or even years down the road. When we worry about the future, we are courting problems without the grace we need to confront the issue, because God hasn't provided for it yet. Jesus instructed, "Don't worry about tomorrow, for tomorrow will bring its own worries. Today's trouble is enough for today" (Matthew 6:34 NLT). God intends for His children to walk by faith, which is developed when we face the day-to-day problems of life and don't have all the answers (2 Corinthians 5:7). God's provision will always arrive on time, but it will seldom come early. As we learn to wait, we grow closer to God, and our trust in Him increases.

> *Father, teach me to walk by faith. As I wait for Your provision, I pray I will grow closer to You and learn to trust You more. Help me to focus on today and have faith in what the future holds.*

4

The love of money is a root
of all kinds of evils. It is
through this craving that
some have wandered away
from the faith and pierced
themselves with many pangs.

1 TIMOTHY 6:10 ESV

*M*oney is a resource that we need to manage with wisdom. Money itself is neither good nor evil, but depending on who is managing it, both good and evil can be accomplished with it. The apostle Paul warned that loving money is the root of all kinds of evil (1 Timothy 6:10). While it's true that money in and of itself isn't evil, some people love money more than they love God, and as a result they wander from the faith and do evil things. When we love anything more than we love God, the object of our affection becomes a dangerous idol that needs to be dismantled. For a Christ follower, the goal of life should not be to become wealthy. The goal in life is to follow Jesus faithfully, wherever He leads us, and to use our lives and all of our resources to bring glory to God.

Father, above all things, my desire is to be faithful and obedient to You. Please help me to have a proper attitude about money and use it for good and never for evil.

5

"What will it profit a man if
he gains the whole world,
and loses his own soul?"

MARK 8:36

I n our culture, it's not uncommon for men and women to invest so much time climbing the corporate ladder that they wreck their health, neglect their family, and ignore their spiritual life. For many of us, a high social standing, financial security, or recognition in a specific field of work is the ultimate goal. But it's possible to attain all of those goals and still feel empty. In a conversation with His disciples, Jesus shared how to live a fulfilled life. He said, "Whoever desires to come after Me, let him deny himself, and take up his cross, and follow Me. For whoever desires to save his life will lose it, but whoever loses his life for My sake and the gospel's will save it" (Mark 8:34–35). In God's economy, those who choose to be self-centered will ultimately miss the best things this life has to offer.[1] But those who follow Christ and live sacrificially for others will experience the best this life has to offer and will have eternal life to look forward to with Christ.

> *Jesus, teach me to follow You closely. I pray I will live wisely during my time on earth and will live in a sacrificial way that brings glory to You and serves others.*

6

Better is a little with
righteousness,
than vast revenues
without justice.

PROVERBS 16:8

*F*or some people, the goal is always to accumulate more: more money, more possessions, more notoriety. There is nothing wrong with abundance, but if the means to acquire more depends on injustice or comes at someone else's expense, then more is not the best option. God cares deeply about our character. If we have poor motives or pursue wealth in a way that reflects a self-serving character, we can be certain that God will discipline us. The author of Hebrews wrote, "The Lord disciplines the one he loves, and he chastens everyone he accepts as his son" (12:6 NIV). For the Christ follower, it is far better to live with less and conduct our affairs with dignity and righteousness than to seek after more and lack justice. Our character is more important than our income, portfolios, and material possessions. The kind of people we are becoming is more valuable than any material thing we possess.

> *Father, I want to have good character and be full of integrity. Help me to remember that my actions are more important than my possessions and to live in a way that brings honor to You.*

7

"If you lend money to
one of my people who
is poor, do not treat him
as a moneylender would.
Charge him nothing for
using your money."

EXODUS 22:25 NCV

The Bible reveals that God cares about the poor, and He opposes those who exploit them. Many times poor people are mistreated because they have few options and lack the means to protest injustice. In terms of lending, poor people routinely pay the highest interest rates and are forced to accept harsh penalties from lenders. But the Scriptures warn about taking advantage of the oppressed. In fact, in the Old Testament God instructed His people to lend without interest to those who are poor (Exodus 22:25). While there is nothing wrong with accumulating wealth, the Scriptures strictly forbid exploiting the poor for material gain (Proverbs 14:31). Those who are wealthy or make a livable wage have a responsibility to advocate for the poor. "Speak up and judge fairly, and defend the rights of the poor and needy" (Proverbs 31:9 NCV). As Christ followers, it is our responsibility to care for the poor and advocate for those who are marginalized.

Father, please increase my compassion for the poor and empower me to advocate for the oppressed. As the Holy Spirit works in my heart, I will become quicker to speak up for those who can't speak for themselves.

8

Do you see a person
skilled in his work?
He will stand in the
presence of kings.
He will not stand in the
presence of the unknown.

PROVERBS 22:29 CSB

A wise person will have more respect for a janitor who does his work with excellence than a doctor who does the bare minimum. As Christians, we are called to do our work with excellence and give our employers or customers our best effort. Sadly, some employees do just enough to get by at their jobs. We all know people who haven't put in a full day's work in months. Shoddy work and mediocre effort are obvious to even a casual observer. But people who take the time and effort to develop great skill in their profession stand out among the rest. The book of Proverbs says, "Do you see a person skilled in his work? He will stand in the presence of kings. He will not stand in the presence of the unknown" (22:29 CSB). Those who work with excellence will be sought after in their fields. Superior work stands out and is rewarded.

> *Father, thank You for my work. Help me to have an excellent work ethic as I do my best and give my full effort to every task.*

9

I have learned to be content
whatever the circumstances.
I know what it is to be in
need, and I know what it is
to have plenty. I have learned
the secret of being content
in any and every situation,
whether well fed or hungry,
whether living in plenty or in
want. I can do all this through
him who gives me strength.

PHILIPPIANS 4:11–13 NIV

*I*n 2017, more than $206 billion was spent on advertising in the United States.[2] The goal of advertising, of course, is to convince consumers to buy specific products. By design, advertising creates a sense of need that suggests a consumer's life will improve if he or she owns specific merchandise. But the Bible's message dramatically differs from that of retailers. The apostle Paul demonstrated that contentment is possible regardless of our circumstances. When he penned his letter to the church at Philippi, he was incarcerated for preaching the gospel. Yet he was able to say with boldness, "I have learned to be content whatever the circumstances" (Philippians 4:11 NIV). Paul understood that contentment could not be bought, because contentment is found only in a relationship with Jesus. Like Paul, if we experience peace with God, we can declare in any situation, "I can do all this through him who gives me strength" (v. 13 NIV).

Lord, You are the only source of real and lasting contentment. Help me to be quick to see that materialism will never satisfy my deepest needs.

10

Jesus entered the Temple and began to drive out all the people buying and selling animals for sacrifice. He knocked over the tables of the money changers and the chairs of those selling doves.

MATTHEW 21:12 NLT

The temple was the focal point of Jewish worship and the place where sojourners came to offer sacrifices to God. Sadly, in Jesus' time unethical merchants had invaded the sacred space with the goal of making an excessive profit. To make matters worse, the vendors had dramatically inflated the costs of the animals they sold, and worshippers were forced to pay as much as ten times the typical cost. Travelers who needed to have their foreign currency exchanged routinely paid a fee of 25 percent.[3] When Jesus entered the temple and saw the appalling scheme, He was so angry He turned over tables and drove the corrupt sellers out of the temple. Worshipping God and treating people fairly should never be compromised for the sake of making a profit. Christians are called to honor God, make an honest living, and treat other people fairly.

Father, as I study Your Word, I learn more about handling all my business dealings with honor and integrity. I pray that my highest priority will be worship. Help me to make an honest living and to treat people fairly.

11

Go to the ant, you sluggard!
Consider her ways
and be wise,
which, having no captain,
overseer or ruler,
provides her supplies
in the summer,
and gathers her food
in the harvest.

PROVERBS 6:6–8

It's tempting to daydream about landing a big account, signing a life-changing contract, or making a huge splash that immediately changes our life. Occasionally something like that happens, but the Bible teaches that overnight success is seldom the way to lasting provision. In the book of Proverbs, the writer points the reader's attention to the ant. Not many of us would consider the ant as something we'd want to imitate. But Solomon instructed the lazy person or someone who is tempted to take shortcuts to consider the habits of the ant (Proverbs 6:6). An ant makes extraordinary progress by consistently doing the work little by little rather than waiting for one big windfall. An ant has the ability to self-motivate and needs no supervision (vv. 7–8). As a result, the ant is well supplied in every season. In our work lives, the sooner we realize there are no shortcuts to success, the quicker we can get on track to achieving our goals one day at a time.

Father, please be with me as I work consistently at the endeavors You have called me to do. Teach me to persevere when I'm tempted to quit, and help me to see my work through until the finish line.

12

"His master answered him, 'You wicked and slothful servant! . . . You ought to have invested my money with the bankers, and at my coming I should have received what was my own with interest.'"

God expects His people to be good stewards of their time, money, and spiritual gifts. In the gospel of Matthew, Jesus told a parable to communicate the importance of investing our skills and talents for the glory of God (25:14–30). In the parable, the first two servants invested wisely and earned a return. The third servant, however, failed to invest what he had been given; as a result, he had no profit for his master. Jesus told this parable to demonstrate that God requires His children to use what He has given them for His glory. Those who are faithful will earn a reward, but those who squander their resources will suffer loss (Matthew 25:29). God has given each believer everything necessary to live a godly life (2 Peter 1:3). If we walk in faith and obey His instructions, we can live a fruitful life that brings glory to God and joy to us (John 15:5).

Father, as I invest my time, knowledge, and spiritual gifts to further Your kingdom on earth, teach me to use my resources wisely and multiply what You have given me for Your glory.

13

"Bring the whole tithe into the storehouse, that there may be food in my house. Test me in this," says the LORD Almighty, "and see if I will not throw open the floodgates of heaven and pour out so much blessing that there will not be room enough to store it."

MALACHI 3:10 NIV

*I*t's not uncommon for some people to cringe at the thought of tithing 10 percent of their income. Of course, God doesn't need our money. After all, He has provided us with everything we possess (1 Corinthians 4:7). But the Bible says that those who withhold their tithes are robbing God (Malachi 3:8). Withholding our tithe demonstrates our lack of faith in God's ability to provide and our unwillingness to contribute to kingdom work. One poll reports that Christians are giving at only 2.5 percent per capita.[4] If every professing believer simply gave the bare minimum, there would be an additional $165 billion for churches to distribute. To put that in context, $25 billion could relieve global hunger, starvation, and preventable diseases in only five years.[5] Tithing is evidence that God's people trust Him to provide and an acknowledgment that He is the sole owner of all things.

> *Father, thank You for the opportunity to financially contribute to Your kingdom work here on earth. Please give me the faith to tithe, and help me to arrange my budget accordingly.*

14

The blessing of the
L<small>ORD</small> makes one rich,
and He adds no
sorrow with it.

PROVERBS 10:22

A lifestyle filled with wealth will be empty apart from God. To complicate things, when we build our own financial empires, the trappings of wealth also bring new burdens and responsibilities. Those who are wealthy often have trouble distinguishing who their genuine friends are from those who are around to ride on their coattails. But the writer of Proverbs said, "The blessing of the LORD makes one rich, and He adds no sorrow with it" (10:22). When God provides us with financial blessing, He does not give begrudgingly or with burdens that deplete our joy. When God provides, there are no strings attached, and His gifts are never tools for manipulation. God's blessings bring joy and never sorrow. Only God can make our life rich. A full bank account doesn't guarantee a lifetime of benefit. Only God can provide the life we are looking for. Anything less is a poor imitation.

> *Father, the blessings You provide come with only joy and no sorrow. Only You can make my life rich, and I pray that You will be my greatest treasure.*

15

Jesus sat near the Temple money box and watched the people put in their money. Many rich people gave large sums of money. Then a poor widow came and put in two small copper coins, which were only worth a few cents.

MARK 12:41–42 NCV

*J*esus was preaching when He warned His audience about religious leaders who liked to be seen in places of honor and who took the best seats in the synagogues. Jesus described them as the type of leaders who take advantage of widows but enjoy calling attention to themselves (Mark 12:38–40). After He finished preaching, Jesus took a seat near the temple money box and watched as people made donations. Among the crowd were wealthy people making substantial contributions, but then a poor widow came and gave two small copper coins (vv. 41–42). Proportionally, the woman contributed far more than the others, because while the wealthy had given out of their surplus, she had given everything she had to live on. Generosity is relative to the circumstance. The reason we withhold money is because we are fearful of lack. But if we trust God with our salvation, we can certainly trust Him with our finances. Giving is a matter of faith.

> *Father, I want to give generously to Your kingdom. Please give me the faith and courage to give sacrificially, just as the poor widow did.*

16

Do not be afraid when
one becomes rich,
when the glory of his
house is increased;
for when he dies he shall
carry nothing away;
his glory shall not
descend after him.

PSALM 49:16–17

It's often been said that we don't bring anything into this world and we can't take anything with us when we go. While we are young, it's easy to get caught up in the things of this world and place too much focus on material possessions. But we will enjoy material wealth only for a limited time, and our souls are built to live for eternity. When we pass from this life to the next, the only thing that will matter is our relationship with Jesus and how we treated other people (Mark 12:30–31). While there's nothing wrong with enjoying nice things, it's essential that we keep our possessions in proper perspective. Things get out of balance when we invest more time tending to our stuff than we do our relationship with God. Billions of years from now, our prized material possessions will have long been in the junkyard, but our souls will still be intact. If we are wise, we will spend ample time in this life preparing to enjoy an eternity that has no end.

Father, I want to have a proper perspective about my material possessions and money. Help me to remember that there is nothing in this world more valuable than You.

17

And whatever you do,
do it heartily, as to the
Lord and not to men.

COLOSSIANS 3:23

It's reported that the typical American employee spends an average of five hours of the workweek on a smartphone, engaged in personal endeavors that are unrelated to work. Most commonly employees are updating social media, checking personal email, watching sports highlights, playing mobile games, and shopping online.[6] The Christian faith calls us to a higher standard in the workplace. The Bible instructs God's people to work hard and put in a full day's effort. According to the Scriptures, a Christian should possess the mind-set that he or she is working for the Lord (Colossians 3:23). We wouldn't dream of attempting to cheat Jesus out of a salary we weren't earning. But millions of professing Christians cheat their employers every day of the workweek. Our work ethic shouldn't be contingent on how we feel about our boss or employer. It should be motivated by our character, and godly character calls for us to put in a full day's work for a full day's pay.

Father, forgive me for the times I've not given my best effort in my workplace. Thank You for my employment, and please help me to develop and maintain an excellent work ethic.

18

The rich rules over the poor,
and the borrower is
servant to the lender.

PROVERBS 22:7

God intends for His people to be free from the burden of sin as well as anything else that has the potential to oppress us. The apostle Paul wrote to the church at Galatia, "Stand fast therefore in the liberty by which Christ has made us free, and do not be entangled again with a yoke of bondage" (Galatians 5:1). When we are strapped with debt, our choices are limited because the main goal is to pay our lenders. The book of Proverbs says, "And the borrower is servant to the lender" (22:7). Christians aren't called to serve lenders; we are called to be servants of Jesus Christ. If we are entangled in debt, we lack the freedom to go anywhere God calls us, because we are shackled to the bills we've accumulated. As consumers, we must be prayerful and wise about the amount of debt we assume. If we find ourselves in excessive debt, it should be our goal to pay it off as soon as possible instead of surrendering to a lifestyle of bondage.

Father, please help me to be wise about the amount of debt I accumulate. I want to serve You and You alone. Help me to get out from under what I owe and to live free from crushing debt.

19

"Sell your possessions and give to the poor. Make money-bags for yourselves that won't grow old, an inexhaustible treasure in heaven, where no thief comes near and no moth destroys."

LUKE 12:33 CSB

*J*esus was speaking to a large crowd of onlookers when He said something startling: "Sell your possessions and give to the poor. Make money-bags for yourselves that won't grow old, an inexhaustible treasure in heaven, where no thief comes near and no moth destroys" (Luke 12:33 CSB). At first, this statement seems contrary to the gospel. After all, isn't salvation by grace through faith and not a result of good deeds (Ephesians 2:8–9)? Indeed, it is. But Jesus offered an important explanation: "For where your treasure is, there your heart will be also" (Luke 12:34). God's salvation is for those who are desperate, humble, and remorseful for their sin. But how a person views material possessions is a barometer of the heart. Anything that competes for an individual's commitment to Christ is a roadblock to salvation. Jesus instructs us to store up our treasure in heaven so that our hearts are set on things above.

Father, Your Word says I can't serve both You and money. I give my heart and my service to You. I pray that there will be no roadblocks that stand in the way of my devotion to You.

20

The law of Your mouth
is better to me
than thousands of coins
of gold and silver.

PSALM 119:72

God's Word is the most valuable asset a Christ follower will ever possess. For the believer, studying the Scriptures is the primary way we develop a vibrant relationship with God, and the Bible serves as the ultimate authority in our life. The psalmist expressed the value of God's Word: "The law of Your mouth is better to me than thousands of coins of gold and silver" (Psalm 119:72). Apart from the Scriptures, it's difficult to have a close relationship with God, but if we immerse ourselves in God's Word, we have the opportunity to know the Lord intimately. God encourages His people to seek Him. Psalm 27:8 says, "When You said, 'Seek My face,' my heart said to You, 'Your face, LORD, I will seek.'" There is nothing more important than knowing the Lord Jesus Christ. The Bible is filled with treasures that can't be purchased in a store. We will do well to manage our financial assets with wisdom, but we should never neglect our greatest treasure of all.

Father, I treasure the incomparable gift of Your Word. As I study it, I pray that You will give me a profound love for the Scriptures and favor to understand what You have said.

21

Do not trust in oppression,
nor vainly hope in robbery;
if riches increase,
do not set your
heart on them.

PSALM 62:10

inancial stability is a worthy endeavor to pursue, but the Scriptures warn about setting our hearts on wealth (Psalm 62:10). In Psalm 62, King David was confronted with people who were abusing their power and oppressing other people by telling lies and spreading falsehood (vv. 3–4). David resolutely chose to wait for God's deliverance (vv. 5–6). He knew that God was his ultimate source of protection, deliverance, and provision. Other people chose to act wickedly, but David resolved to trust God. There are multiple situations in life when even large sums of money and powerful connections cannot help us. But God is in control of every situation, and He has the power to change any circumstance. David warned, "Do not trust in oppression, nor vainly hope in robbery; if riches increase, do not set your heart on them" (v. 10). Money has limitations, but God does not. It's foolish to set our hearts on riches, but it's wise to set our hearts on God.

Father, I trust You in every circumstance. I pray that I will be a good steward of my finances and that I will be mindful that while money has limited ability to help, You are in control of all things.

22

But those who won't
care for their relatives,
especially those in their own
household, have denied the
true faith. Such people are
worse than unbelievers.

1 TIMOTHY 5:8 NLT

In the New Testament, the early church often cared for widows in need but soon found that it couldn't support everyone seeking assistance.[7] As a result, criteria were put in place to assess who was the most vulnerable (1 Timothy 5:4–8). It was determined that the widows who had children and grandchildren capable of helping should look first to their family for financial support, and the church would care for those who had no family to help them. Parents spend the first years of their children's lives investing time, money, and resources into raising their kids. God is pleased when adult children make a return offering to their parents (1 Timothy 5:4). Love and compassion are at the core of the Christian faith. If we deny our parents love and compassion, our salvation remains intact but we have denied some of the basic principles of the Christian faith.

Father, please give me the ability to care for my family members in the same way they have cared for me. I ask for opportunities to extend kindness and generosity to those in need among my family.

23

Some trust in chariots
and some in horses,
but we trust in the name
of the LORD our God.

PSALM 20:7 ESV

$\mathcal{A}$s we look ahead to retirement, it's not uncommon to worry about the future. People are living longer lives, which is a good thing, but it comes with the added concern that retirement money will run out. The Bible has plenty to say about wise financial stewardship, and Christians are to plan responsibly for the future. Ultimately, however, believers are called to entrust themselves to God. Our faith shouldn't rest in our 401(k) plans, portfolios, mutual funds, or stocks and bonds. After all, it's possible to lose all of our financial assets in the blink of an eye. Certainly, we must be wise with our money. But we can never lose sight of the fact that God is our ultimate source of provision. The psalmist wrote, "Some trust in chariots and some in horses, but we trust in the name of the LORD our God" (Psalm 20:7 ESV). Rather than trusting in assets that can be lost, we should trust God, who will never fail us.

God, thank You for Your constant faithfulness. I will be mindful that You are my ultimate source of security. Help me to plan wisely for the future and to always entrust myself to You.

24

"Do not go over your vineyard a second time or pick up the grapes that have fallen. Leave them for the poor and the foreigner. I am the LORD your God."

LEVITICUS 19:10 NIV

*I*n the Old Testament, there were laws and customs in place that provided for the poor. At harvesttime, the field owners were commanded to go over their vineyards only one time and to leave any produce that had been left behind for poor people, immigrants, and refugees. Doing so gave those who were in need an opportunity to gather their own food without being forced to beg. Gathering their food demanded effort on their behalf and kept their dignity intact. Because all landowners were required to leave behind a small portion of their harvest, no one individual or group was burdened with the huge task, because everyone assumed some responsibility. The Scriptures repeatedly demonstrate that God intends for His people to care for the poor, marginalized, and oppressed. Caring for the poor is not a task that should be delegated only to the government or one group or organization. All God's people are summoned to care for those in need.

> *Father, I pray You will give me Your care and concern for those in need. I ask that You will give me a heart filled with compassion and hands that are quick to offer help.*

25

Be diligent to know the
state of your flocks,
and attend to your herds.

PROVERBS 27:23

*B*eing wise stewards of our resources demands that we pay close attention to our work and everything related to our fields of business. In the Old Testament, people commonly made a living as shepherds and farmers. So it's not surprising that the author of Proverbs instructed his readers to be diligent about their flocks. In modern times, not as many of us are employed as shepherds or farmers, but the point remains the same. Good stewards are attentive and constantly aware of what is transpiring in their workplace. It's wise to pay close attention so we can be proactive in addressing problems before things get out of hand and to avoid being caught off guard. If we are aware of what's happening, we can anticipate future needs and make plans in advance. Knowing the state of our flocks isn't a task that should be delegated. It's our responsibility to stay alert and to take responsibility for every aspect of our personal and work lives.

> *Father, give me wisdom in my work life. Teach me to remain alert, to pay close attention, and to anticipate needs. I thank You for my work and pray for Your blessing.*

26

Lord, who may abide in
your tabernacle? . . .
He who does not put out
his money at usury,
nor does he take a bribe
against the innocent.
He who does these things
shall never be moved.

PSALM 15:1, 5

*D*uring Old Testament times, it wasn't uncommon for people to need to borrow money after a year of failed crops. The laws of the Pentateuch didn't regulate commercial loans but rather placed stipulations on individuals who might lend money to a friend or neighbor who needed a loan to buy seed or to meet another pressing need.[8] In these instances, the people of Israel were forbidden to charge interest to their fellow Israelites. Similarly, Israelites were forbidden from taking bribes against the innocent. Justice is a trait that should characterize God's people. There is no place in the Christian faith for dishonesty, greed, or injustice. When a friend or neighbor is experiencing hard times, Christ followers should view it as an opportunity to help rather than a chance to make a profit. Christians should be the most grace-filled and kindest people in our communities.

Father, thank You for all the ways You have demonstrated Your grace and kindness to me. Help me to be quick to extend grace and compassion to anyone in need.

27

In all labor there is profit,
but idle chatter leads
only to poverty.

PROVERBS 14:23

$\mathcal{P}$rocrastination is the enemy of productivity. While it's wise to spend some time contemplating and planning a project, at some point we must finish our planning and stop talking so the work gets done. Today's scripture issues a warning for those who would rather talk about work than do it. Labor and idle chatter are on opposite ends of the spectrum, and engaging in one or the other will lead to very different outcomes. While all types of work will produce varying degrees of profit, those who choose a lifestyle of idle chatter will become poor. God intends for all human beings to be productive either at home or in the workplace. Work brings us not only profit but also a sense of accomplishment and purpose that merely talking about a task can never provide.

Father, thank You for creating me with the intention of giving me work to do. As I concentrate on having a strong work ethic, enable me to do my work with a good attitude.

28

Do not worry about anything,
but pray and ask God
for everything you need,
always giving thanks.

PHILIPPIANS 4:6 NCV

*A*ccording to a recent poll, money is the number one stressor among Americans. Among those surveyed, more than 40 percent reported feeling worried about saving for retirement and the possibility of outliving their savings.[9] Fear and worry are topics that are addressed repeatedly in the Bible. God knows human beings are prone to worry; therefore, the Scriptures have plenty to say about the issue. According to the Scriptures, the cure for worry is prayer. Paul instructed his readers to pray rather than worry. Anxiety can cause serious damage to our bodies, but it doesn't have the ability to improve our circumstances. When we are tempted to worry, we can interrupt those anxious thoughts with prayer. If we do, we will experience peace. Paul concluded, "And God's peace, which is so great we cannot understand it, will keep your hearts and minds in Christ Jesus" (Philippians 4:7 NCV).

> *Father, please help me to develop a powerful prayer life. I want to replace my fear with faith. Teach me to pray when I am worried and to live in Your peace.*

29

They did not demand
to know how the money
was spent, because the
workers were honest.

2 KINGS 12:15 NCV

*D*uring King Jehoash's reign, he did what was right in the sight of the Lord (2 Kings 12:2). The king was dissatisfied that the temple was in poor shape, and he ordered the priests to collect money to make repairs (vv. 4–5). After a long delay, during a time when little was getting done, King Jehoash ordered the priests a second time to repair the temple, but he forbade them from collecting additional funds (v. 7). Finally, the money was distributed to the carpenters and builders who did the work.

Whether or not we realize it, we are known for our actions (Proverbs 20:11). As Christ followers, we should be the kind of people who can be trusted with money. Dishonesty and greed are not traits that characterize the Christian life.

> *Father, I know it is important to You that Your followers have excellent character. I long to be someone who can be trusted. Help me to be honest and faithful in all my dealings.*

30

There will never cease to be
poor people in the land; that
is why I am commanding you,
"Open your hand willingly
to your poor and needy
brother in your land."

DEUTERONOMY 15:11 CSB

oth Moses and Jesus said the poor would always be among us (Deuteronomy 15:11; Matthew 26:11). With this in mind, Moses said, "That is why I am commanding you, 'Open your hand willingly to your poor and needy brother in your land'" (Deuteronomy 15:11b CSB). Because the poor will always be among us, we need to adopt a lifestyle of caring for those in need. It's tempting to make a onetime donation or serve in a soup kitchen around the holidays and believe we've done our part. Although that's a great place to start, the poor need help on a consistent basis. No one person, church, or organization can meet all the needs in the community, so it's imperative that every believer do his or her part. "Opening our hand" to the poor might mean providing a meal or making a financial donation, but it also might mean assisting with job placement, volunteering at a local shelter, or working to put infrastructures in place that alleviate poverty.

Father, please show me my part and how I can best serve the poor. I want to be part of the solution to alleviate suffering in my generation.

31

The LORD makes poor
and makes rich;
He brings low and lifts up.

1 SAMUEL 2:7

For years, Hannah was grief-stricken as she struggled with infertility (1 Samuel 1:5–7). But when Hannah prayed for a child, God answered her and she gave birth to Samuel (v. 20). When it came time to dedicate Samuel to the Lord, Hannah prayed, "The LORD makes poor and makes rich; He brings low and lifts up" (2:7). Hannah's suffering and the long wait for a child had taught her about the sovereignty of God. She had learned by experience that although she had no control over whether she would ever conceive, God was in complete control of her circumstances. Hannah realized that this truth extends to every aspect of life, even to our ability to create wealth. There is no such thing as a "self-made" man or woman. If we experience any degree of financial abundance, it's because the Lord has shown us His favor.

Father, help me to remember that You are sovereign over all things. I entrust myself to Your plan for my life, and I will wait patiently for You to reveal Your will.

32

[God] saves the needy
from the sword,
from the mouth of
the mighty,
and from their hand.
So the poor have hope,
and injustice shuts her mouth.

JOB 5:15–16

*T*ime and again in the Scriptures, we see God coming to the aid of someone who is down-and-out. Job was experiencing a heartache few of us could imagine. His children had died unexpectedly, his home and property were destroyed, his health was failing, his wife had urged him to curse God over their troubles, and his friends were questioning if Job had brought this string of calamity on himself (Job 1:13–2:13). Understandably, Job was so distraught that he lamented the day he was born (3:3). But the book of Job reminds us that God intervenes on behalf of the needy (5:15). God provides what His people need in every season of life. In some seasons, we need comfort and hope. Other times we need financial provision or a new opportunity to arise. God is faithful to deliver. After a terrible season of loss, God restored Job. After all that Job had been through, he said, "I know that You can do everything, and that no purpose of Yours can be withheld from You" (42:2).

> *Father, teach me to trust You with my family, my health, and my finances. Help me to remember that nothing is outside of Your control and that Your purposes cannot fail.*

33

God will never forget
the needy;
the hope of the afflicted
will never perish.

PSALM 9:18 NIV

*I*n 2016, more than 12 percent of the American population lived in poverty.[10] Even worse, 18 percent of American children live below the poverty line and reside in homes with unstable food supplies. Surprisingly, more than 50 percent of those seeking emergency assistance for hunger at local food banks are employed, so many of those impacted are among the working poor. In a prosperous American culture, it's easy for the middle and upper classes to overlook the poor or look down on them and assume they are destitute because of a lifetime of bad choices, but that's not always true. Regardless of the reasons for poverty, the Bible teaches that God's people have a responsibility to help. The psalmist wrote, "God will never forget the needy; the hope of the afflicted will never perish" (Psalm 9:18 NIV). All people are made in the image of God and therefore are worthy of our care. God hasn't forgotten the poor. As His servants, neither should we.

Father, I want to be a part of the solution to world hunger. Teach me ways that I can help and provide long-term solutions for those in need. Thank You, Lord, for the way You have provided for me.

34

A good man leaves
an inheritance to his
children's children,
but the wealth of the sinner is
stored up for the righteous.

PROVERBS 13:22

The book of Proverbs is filled with wisdom, counsel, and godly insight that instructs readers in wise living. Unlike other books of the Bible, the book of Proverbs shares principles that are true in many cases but not in every instance. For instance, Proverbs teaches that God blesses the righteous, and that careful planning will allow a wise steward to have enough to leave to his or her children and grandchildren. This is one of those principles that is true in many cases, but there are exceptions. Most of us know godly people who never became wealthy enough to leave behind an inheritance for their family. But even when godly people don't accumulate enough wealth to pass on to future generations, they can pass on a spiritual inheritance that is even more valuable than money. Godly parents and grandparents have the potential to make great spiritual deposits in their family line that will make an incalculable impact for generations to come.

Father, I pray I will be a wise steward of all my assets. I ask You to teach me to invest in my children and grandchildren and leave them a godly inheritance.

35

"Who would begin construction of a building without first calculating the cost to see if there is enough money to finish it? Otherwise, you might complete only the foundation before running out of money, and then everyone would laugh at you. They would say, 'There's the person who started that building and couldn't afford to finish it!'"

LUKE 14:28–30 NLT

esus was preaching to a large crowd and teaching them what it meant to be His disciple. During His earthly ministry, Jesus never sugarcoated what it meant to follow Him, and He encouraged His people to count the cost of discipleship. As He was speaking, Jesus used an illustration of constructing a building and pointed out that before beginning construction, a wise person would make an estimate of what it would cost to complete the task (Luke 14:28–30). Jesus calls for honest appraisal in every area of our life. The Christian life demands that we be people who engage in self-examination in our spiritual lives, marriages, finances, and career. Our finances are closely connected to our spiritual lives because our spending habits are a barometer of our priorities. If we fail to "count the cost," we have the potential to engage in projects we can't finish. Wise living demands we consider the cost, make an honest appraisal, and make informed decisions.

Father, please give me wisdom for every aspect of life. I want to make good choices and plan ahead. Keep me from poor choices, and fill me with Your knowledge and wisdom.

36

The plans of the diligent
lead surely to plenty,
but those of everyone who
is hasty, surely to poverty.

PROVERBS 21:5

The first thing God reveals about Himself in Scripture is that He is working (Genesis 1:1). As human beings created in the image of God, we too are built for work (v. 26). All people are designed to be productive human beings who contribute to our households and communities. The book of Proverbs instructs readers, "The plans of the diligent lead surely to plenty, but those of everyone who is hasty, surely to poverty" (21:5). Approaching our work with diligence leads to a successful outcome, but those who do their job sloppily to get it done as quickly as possible will be left wanting. Most Americans who work full-time invest a minimum of forty hours each week in the workplace, which is nearly 25 percent of the week. Since our work lives represent such a large portion of our time, it's imperative that we work diligently so we can enjoy the best possible outcomes.

> *Lord, please help me to approach my work with diligence. Teach me to give my best effort even when I don't feel like doing the work so that I will have an excellent work ethic.*

37

"For the oppression
of the poor, for the
sighing of the needy,
now I will arise,"
says the Lord;
"I will set him in the safety
for which he yearns."

PSALM 12:5

God keeps a watchful eye and is constantly aware of what is transpiring. As children of God, we never have to wonder if He knows what is taking place. When the Egyptians were oppressing the Israelites, the Lord said, "I know their sorrows" (Exodus 3:7). God knows our situations more intimately than we do, and He comes to the aid of those in need. "'For the oppression of the poor, for the sighing of the needy, Now I will arise,' says the LORD; 'I will set him in the safety for which he yearns'" (Psalm 12:5). God acted on behalf of the Israelites, and He is faithful to intervene for those who are poor and oppressed. At any given moment, the Lord is aware of how we are being treated, and He knows exactly how we treat others.

Father, if I experience oppression, I pray You will come to my aid. Please make me quick to come to the aid of others.

38

"Woe to him who builds his
house by unrighteousness
and his chambers by injustice,
who uses his neighbor's
service without wages
and gives him nothing
for his work."

JEREMIAH 22:13

E mployers and managers in the workplace have a biblical responsibility to treat their employees with justice and dignity. In biblical times, it wasn't uncommon for employers to hire day laborers who were paid their salary at the end of every shift. These workers lived day to day and were at the mercy of the bosses who paid them. But some of the employers were unjust and hired laborers to do the work and then failed to pay their wages (Jeremiah 22:13). This morally corrupt practice undoubtedly caused families to go hungry. Christian employers and managers should be the kindest and most competent bosses in the workplace. God commands His people, "Do justice and righteousness, and deliver from the hand of the oppressor him who has been robbed" (Jeremiah 22:3 ESV).

> *Lord, managing people is a huge task. Help me to treat others with dignity, kindness, and integrity and to anticipate their needs in a way that brings You glory.*

39

The generous soul
will be made rich,
and he who waters will
also be watered himself.

PROVERBS 11:25

The world's economy measures success by how much we can accumulate. But in God's economy, success is measured by our generosity. Solomon wrote, "The generous soul will be made rich, and he who waters will also be watered himself" (Proverbs 11:25). Throughout Scripture there is a consistent theme of God blessing His people so they can be a blessing to others. God said to Abraham, "I will bless you and make your name great; and you shall be a blessing" (Genesis 12:2). God intends for His people to be channels of His blessing. Rather than being depleted by giving, we are replenished as we give. This attitude permeated the New Testament church. When the apostle Paul addressed the elders at the church of Ephesus, he said, "In all things I have shown you that by working hard in this way we must help the weak and remember the words of the Lord Jesus, how he himself said, 'It is more blessed to give than to receive'" (Acts 20:35 ESV).

> *Father, help me to remember that I am to be a channel of Your blessings. I know I will grow in generosity and will experience joy each time I give.*

40

"If one of your brethren
becomes poor, and falls
into poverty among you,
then you shall help him, like
a stranger or a sojourner,
that he may live with you."

LEVITICUS 25:35

*I*n biblical times, people often counted on hospitality from others in their faith communities. In the book of Leviticus, Israelites were instructed to show mercy to one another because they had been recipients of God's mercy. In modern times, there is less of an emphasis placed on hospitality, but it's still a crucial aspect of biblical fellowship. Opening our homes for Bible study, for fellowship, or to someone in need of a place to stay is a tangible way we show each other the love of Christ. Everything we possess has been given to us by God, and that includes our homes and possessions. In his first letter to the church at Corinth, Paul asked, "What do you have that you did not receive?" (1 Corinthians 4:7). When we understand that everything we have has been gifted to us by God, and ultimately belongs to Him, we will be quick to open our homes to those who are in need.

Father, everything I possess ultimately belongs to You. I long to be generous with the gifts You have given me, and I pray I will show godly hospitality.

41

The poor shall eat
and be satisfied;
those who seek Him
will praise the LORD.
Let your heart live forever!

PSALM 22:26

Regardless of our income bracket, we are spiritually destitute apart from Christ. But the good news of the gospel teaches that all who follow Jesus as Lord are reconciled to the Father and called children of God (John 1:12; 14:6). The psalmist depicted an image of a feast that would've resonated with a Jewish audience because it was a picture of the anticipated messianic kingdom.[11] "The poor shall eat and be satisfied; those who seek Him will praise the LORD. Let your heart live forever!" (Psalm 22:26). A time is coming when all God's people, both rich and poor, will feast at the marriage supper of the Lamb (Revelation 19:9). At that time we will be in the presence of Christ, and there will be no more suffering, heartache, or tears (21:4). The trials of this life will be a memory, and we will be forever satisfied.

Father, apart from You I am destitute. I eagerly anticipate the time when all Your people will be with You for eternity, and there will be no more tears or suffering.

42

Through wisdom a
house is built,
and by understanding
it is established;
by knowledge the
rooms are filled
with all precious and
pleasant riches.

PROVERBS 24:3–4

*I*n the Scriptures, wisdom is portrayed as valuable as precious treasure and riches. We all know of foolish people who lost a great deal of wealth due to unwise choices. But God gives wisdom to those of us who ask. The book of James says, "If any of you lacks wisdom, let him ask of God, who gives to all liberally and without reproach, and it will be given to him" (1:5). God's wisdom guides us in building a good and productive life and a way of living that is admirable. "Through wisdom a house is built, and by understanding it is established; by knowledge the rooms are filled with all precious and pleasant riches" (Proverbs 24:3–4). We need wisdom to be good stewards of our money, time, and resources. It's an excellent habit to continually ask God for more wisdom. The Scriptures instruct us to ask, and if we do, we can be confident that God will provide the wisdom we need.

Father, please make me wiser than I am and teach me things I couldn't know apart from You. Teach me to steward my resources in a way that is pleasing to You.

43

Then Jesus said to the apostles, "When I sent you out without a purse, a bag, or sandals, did you need anything?" They said, "No."

LUKE 22:35 NCV

When Jesus sent out His disciples on a preaching tour, He instructed them to take little to nothing with them (Luke 9:3). The Twelve had been given the power to heal diseases and alleviate suffering, but they were not to collect money or acquire wealth at the expense of those who were suffering. Jesus instructed them, "You received without paying; give without pay" (Matthew 10:8 ESV). Jesus wanted the disciples not only to avoid taking advantage of the sick but also to live by faith and trust Him for their daily needs. Later, when the spiritual climate of Israel was changing and Christ's death on the cross was imminent, Jesus pointed back to that time as a teaching tool to remind the disciples that God had always provided for their needs. Jesus knew things would change after His death and resurrection, and people would not be as receptive to the disciples' teaching.[12] But God is our provider, and regardless of what is going on in modern culture, we can trust Him to provide.

> *Father, thank You for being my provider. Help me to be mindful that I can always rely on You to meet my needs.*

44

"Why do you spend money
for what is not bread,
and your wages for what
does not satisfy?
Listen carefully to Me,
and eat what is good,
and let your soul delight
itself in abundance."

ISAIAH 55:2

*A*n incalculable amount of money is spent each year by people who are trying to fill a spiritual void with material possessions. All of us know what it's like to feel sad or depressed and purchase something we don't need in an effort to feel better. Human beings have longings and voids that only God can fill. The good news is that the Lord invites us into a relationship: "Come, everyone who thirsts, come to the waters; and he who has no money, come, buy and eat! Come, buy wine and milk without money and without price" (Isaiah 55:1 ESV). When we lack a vibrant relationship with God, we attempt to fill the void with things that have no ability to satisfy our needs. But God longs for us to be in relationship with Him and live in His peace. "Listen carefully to Me, and eat what is good, and let your soul delight itself in abundance" (v. 2).

> *Father, You meet my deepest longings and needs. Give me wisdom to know when I am attempting to fill a void only You can fill.*

45

Blessed is he who
considers the poor;
the LORD will deliver him
in time of trouble.

PSALM 41:1

King David wrote, "Blessed is he who considers the poor" (Psalm 41:1). In this context, the term *poor* refers to those who are helpless and in a difficult situation and depending on others. To "consider" means to be attentive to their needs and be willing to help.[13] As the king of Israel, David was undoubtedly aware of the challenges of the poor, and there is good reason to believe he treated them with kindness and integrity. David enjoyed a long history with God and witnessed the Lord respond in countless circumstances. Of those who considered the poor, David said, "The LORD will deliver him in time of trouble" (Psalm 41:1). God honors those who show kindness to the weak and help those who are unable to pay back a favor. God's people should be kind to the poor because the Bible commands it, but doing so also pleases God and invites His blessing.

> *Father, help me to remember to be kind to the poor and to treat those in need with integrity and compassion. I want to be quick to help those who can't repay.*

46

He is not partial to princes,
nor does He regard the
rich more than the poor;
for they are all the
work of His hands.

JOB 34:19

Western culture puts a high premium on celebrities, the wealthy and beautiful, and those who are in the public eye. Thankfully, God doesn't show favoritism. God views all people—young and old, rich and poor, successful and struggling—as "the work of His hands" (Job 34:19). Our identity doesn't rest on our bank accounts, our external appearance, or the amount of success we have achieved in our field of work. Society doesn't have the authority to assign our worth. Our worth was settled at Calvary. Jesus viewed us as valuable enough to die for, and our worth was settled by His sacrifice (Romans 5:8). As God's people, we too should value other people based on the fact that they are made in the image of God. The Bible warns against showing partiality (James 2:1–4). If God doesn't regard the rich more favorably than He does the poor, then neither should His people.

> *Father, please give me Your love for other people. Teach me to view all people as men and women made in Your image so that I will show no favoritism but kindness to all.*

47

The rich and the poor
have this in common,
the Lord is the maker
of them all.

PROVERBS 22:2

At some point you've likely heard the phrase "We don't have anything in common." When someone makes that statement, it usually means the person he or she is referring to has different tastes or doesn't enjoy similar things. While it's true that God created humanity with remarkable diversity, we have more in common with other people than we might expect. All people have a strong desire to be loved, heard, valued, and safe. No one likes to be disrespected or treated poorly. It might be tempting to think that a billionaire has nothing in common with a homeless man living on the streets, but that's not true. The author of today's scripture from Proverbs wrote that God made all of them. Wealth and poverty have the ability to categorize neighborhoods, status, and opportunity, but neither wealth nor poverty can take away the fact that we are all created by God and long for the same basic things.

Father, thank You for connecting all human beings through the commonality of being made in Your image. Help me to remember that we are more alike than different.

48

Do not take advantage of
a hired worker who is poor
and needy, whether that
worker is a fellow Israelite
or a foreigner residing
in one of your towns.

DEUTERONOMY 24:14 NIV

Immigration has been a topic of hot debate in recent times. The Bible has a lot to say about how God's people are to treat immigrants. The Scriptures forbid employers from taking advantage of workers, regardless of whether they are natural-born citizens or immigrants from a foreign country. According to today's scripture, the point is that poor people and immigrant employees should be treated with the same justice as other workers. Employers are not to take advantage of the fact that the poor, needy, and disenfranchised are vulnerable and unable to advocate for themselves. Regardless of social status, race, or background, all people are to be treated fairly. When we demonstrate a lack of justice to the poor and vulnerable, we provoke the ire of God (Jeremiah 22:13).

> *Lord, I pray I will treat all people with justice, dignity, and respect. When I witness injustice, I ask for the wisdom and favor to advocate for the powerless who can't speak up for themselves.*

49

Better is a poor but wise youth than an old but foolish king who no longer pays attention to warnings.

ECCLESIASTES 4:13 CSB

Old age is a gift that isn't granted to everyone, but those who are advanced in years are sometimes at risk of closing their hearts, ears, and minds to instruction. Foolish people assume their experience has taught them everything they need to know. No matter how old we are, there is always an opportunity to learn new things. Solomon is considered the wisest man who ever lived, and he knew that old age didn't guarantee wisdom and that even young people have the potential to possess great wisdom. Ideally, the older we get, the wiser we will become. But to grow in wisdom, we must remain open and humble to learning. God is faithful to increase our wisdom, but we must continue to seek it all the days of our life.

Father, I will seek Your wisdom in every season of life. Continue to teach me so that I will continue to learn new things deep into my old age.

50

The crown of the wise
is their riches,
but the foolishness
of fools is folly.

PROVERBS 14:24

$\mathcal{W}$isdom is at the top of the list when it comes to valuable things money can't buy. No one wants to be a fool, but how many of us are intentionally seeking to become wiser? Proverbs says that the crown of the wise is their riches. In this context, a "crown" is anything that visibly gives public honor.[14] Wise people can enjoy their wealth because they aren't motivated by greed. Fools, however, continue on a self-defeating path that leads nowhere. Greed is foolish, but it is wise to strive to continually increase in wisdom. Solomon wrote, "For wisdom is better than rubies, and all the things one may desire cannot be compared with her" (Proverbs 8:11). Wisdom can't be bought, but acquiring wisdom makes us wise in money management and every other area of life.

> *Lord, please guard my heart against greed and help me to be motivated to grow in wisdom. I will seek it like a treasure.*

51

"Six days you shall do your work, and on the seventh day you shall rest, that your ox and your donkey may rest, and the son of your female servant and the stranger may be refreshed."

EXODUS 23:12

*M*odern culture moves at breakneck speed. Most of us have overbooked schedules that leave little room for rest and refilling. As a result, scores of people get out of bed every morning feeling exhausted and on the verge of burnout. God designed the human body for both work and rest. In the creation account, God modeled what it looked like to work six days and rest on the seventh (Genesis 2:2). God didn't need to rest, because He never tires or grows weary (Isaiah 40:28). But God modeled a Sabbath rest for us to imitate. When we are busy with our careers and raising children, there is a temptation to work seven days a week, but that's a recipe for burnout. In the same way that we trust God with our finances, we must also trust Him with our time. As the designer of the human body, God knows what we need to function at our highest capacity, and that includes a weekly Sabbath rest.

> *Father, thank You for the gift of rest. Help me to manage my schedule in a way that makes rest a priority so that I can function at my highest capacity.*

52

Jesus told him, "If you want to be perfect, go and sell all your possessions and give the money to the poor, and you will have treasure in heaven. Then come, follow me."

MATTHEW 19:21 NLT

The gospel of Matthew tells the story of a rich young man who came to talk to Jesus and asked, "Teacher, what good deed must I do to have eternal life?" (Matthew 19:16 NLT). Jesus responded by telling the man to keep all the commandments. Of course it's impossible for any of us to keep all the commandments perfectly, but failing at keeping the law opens our eyes to our need for a Savior. Sadly, the young man missed Jesus' point because he wrongly assumed he had kept all the commandments since his youth. But Jesus knew his heart, so He told him to sell all of his possessions and give them to the poor (v. 21). The rich young man went away sad because he was wealthy and not willing to part with his possessions. To follow Christ as Lord, we have to be willing to forsake everything. God doesn't always ask us to forfeit our possessions, but He knows our hearts and whether we are willing to walk away from wealth to follow Jesus.

> Lord, I pray I will love You above all things. Please point out areas in my life where I place too much emphasis on materialism, and give me a heart that treasures You above everything else.

53

The rich man's wealth
is his strong city,
and like a high wall in
his own esteem.

PROVERBS 18:11

To a degree, it's true that wealth provides a certain amount of protection that the poverty-stricken are unable to access. For instance, money can purchase high-quality health care, a good education, and the opportunity to live in a safer neighborhood. For this reason, the author of Proverbs said, "The rich man's wealth is his strong city, and like a high wall in his own esteem" (18:11). But in every instance, money has limitations, and it's common to overestimate what money can do. Even billionaires aren't insulated from suffering. It's possible to have access to the best doctors in the world and still die from disease. An Ivy League education won't protect from a stock market crash. A gated community can't always keep evil away from the front door. God is the only one who can't fail us. Money has the ability to purchase comfort and a degree of security, but ultimately God is our only trustworthy source of protection.

> *Father, help me to remember that You are my ultimate source of security. You are the only One who can never fail. Teach me to entrust myself to You and You alone.*

54

Yours is the kingdom, O Lord,
and You are exalted
as head over all.
Both riches and honor
come from You,
and You reign over all.

1 CHRONICLES 29:11–12

ultiple publications each year list the richest people in the world. Often the names are familiar because they've been among the wealthiest people and have had a high profile for many years. Those on the list are always the highest achievers in their fields, and they enjoy notoriety among peers and strangers alike. But the Bible insists that the ability to generate wealth is a gift from God: "Both riches and honor come from You, and You reign over all" (1 Chronicles 29:12). Some of the wealthiest people in the world do not even believe God exists, but that doesn't mean that He isn't the source of their gain. Scripture says that God "reign[s] over all" (v. 12). That includes believers and nonbelievers. Apart from God's favor, it is impossible to accumulate wealth. If we have food in the pantry, have money in the bank, or find ourselves among the world's wealthiest people, it's because God has made it possible.

> *Lord, I acknowledge that both wealth and honor come from You. Because You are exalted above all things, I will be mindful that You are the source of all my gains.*

55

And He said to them, "Render therefore to Caesar the things that are Caesar's, and to God the things that are God's."

MATTHEW 22:21

*F*ew things are more deflating than studying a paycheck stub and realizing how much money has been deducted for taxes. It might be possible to search the world over and never find a single person who enjoys paying a tax bill. During Jesus' earthly ministry, the Pharisees were plotting how to trap Jesus by luring Him to say something they could use to condemn Him, so they asked Jesus if it was lawful to pay taxes to Caesar. Taxes were a controversial issue in Israel since some Jews believed paying taxes to a pagan contradicted God's authority over His people. Jesus responded, "Render therefore to Caesar the things that are Caesar's, and to God the things that are God's" (Matthew 22:21). Jesus didn't come to establish a political kingdom that opposed Caesar, so God's people are to obey civil laws and pay taxes. God's Word calls us to be upstanding citizens in our communities, and part of our responsibility as citizens is to pay taxes.

> *Father, because I want to be a good neighbor and an upstanding citizen in the community, I ask You to help me have a good attitude about my civic responsibilities.*

56

He who oppresses the poor
to increase his riches,
and he who gives to the rich,
will surely come to poverty.

PROVERBS 22:16

*I*t's no coincidence that the poor areas in every town are the most densely populated by pawn shops, rent-to-own furniture stores, and places that offer cash advances on future paychecks. These types of businesses offer poor people the opportunity to borrow or do business without a good credit record, but they charge outrageous interest rates and service charges. The Bible warns about taking advantage of the poor: "He who oppresses the poor to increase his riches . . . will surely come to poverty" (Proverbs 22:16). God opposes those who take advantage of the vulnerable. While there is nothing wrong with making a profit, it is morally corrupt to profit from those who are oppressed and marginalized. God cares about our business methods, and charging exorbitant interest to people who barely get by is not the characteristic of someone whose heart has been transformed by the gospel.

> *Father, I want to love the things You love and hate the things You hate. Give me a holy disdain for any business method that mistreats the poor and vulnerable.*

57

Keep your life free from love of money, and be content with what you have, for he has said, "I will never leave you nor forsake you."

HEBREWS 13:5 ESV

*F*or better or worse, our greatest desires become the driving forces of our lives. That's why the writer of today's scripture warned his readers against the love of money. If money is our greatest love, then acquiring wealth will be our strongest motivator, and we will ultimately trust in the uncertainty of money rather than the all-powerful God of the universe. It is not wrong to earn or possess large sums of money. The Bible identifies a number of wealthy people who loved and honored God above all things. But if we value our finances more than we value God, we have fallen into dangerous idolatry. Our greatest security doesn't rest in our bank accounts. It rests in the presence of God, who has promised never to leave or forsake His people.

> *Lord, please give me a proper perspective about money. With Your guidance I will be a wise steward of what You entrust to me, but I will put my ultimate hope in You.*

58

A little that a
righteous man has
is better than the riches
of many wicked.

PSALM 37:16

*H*ave you ever wondered why godless people seem to prosper while the righteous suffer? King David addressed the issue in Psalm 37, where he reminded his readers not to be discouraged by people who engage in evil and immoral practices: "Do not fret because of evildoers, nor be envious of the workers of iniquity. For they shall soon be cut down like the grass, and wither as the green herb" (vv. 1–2). David reminds us that regardless of the way things look, it's far better to remain faithful to God. The Lord will be faithful to deal with every injustice and people who practice evil. It may temporarily seem as if the wicked are getting away with their behavior, but the Bible assures us they are not. God's people are far better off obeying His rules, even if it means temporarily having less.

> *Father, help me to obey Your Word regardless of the cost. I will not be discouraged by those who practice evil because I know You are a God of justice.*

59

Better is the poor who
walks in his integrity
than one who is perverse
in his lips, and is a fool.

PROVERBS 19:1

*G*odly integrity is more valuable than a multi-digit financial portfolio. Honesty, goodwill, and following through with what we say we will do should characterize every person who professes faith in Christ. God's preferences and values differ from the world's. "Better is the poor who walks with his integrity than one who is perverse in his lips, and is a fool" (Proverbs 19:1). Of course, no one desires to live in poverty. But the Scriptures teach that being poor but honest is more desirable than being a perverse fool. Fools are difficult to help because they always believe they are right and refuse to take advice (12:15). Money is little help to a fool because he is his own worst enemy and eventually does himself great harm. But a poor person with integrity can make significant progress. Our finances can change overnight, but good character will always remain intact as a valuable asset.

> *Lord, help me to be honest and filled with goodwill toward other people. I want to be a person known to follow through with my commitments and to be someone others can trust.*

60

Everyone who thirsts,
come to the waters;
and you who have no money,
come, buy and eat.
Yes, come, buy wine and milk
without money and
without price.

ISAIAH 55:1

If a person is hungry or thirsty for a long time, it becomes difficult to think of anything else. Our bodies are dependent on water and food, and without those basic resources, we quickly become physically and emotionally depleted. It's no accident that the prophet Isaiah used hunger and thirst as a metaphor when extending an invitation to experience the blessings of God. Apart from a relationship with Christ, we experience a hollow void that dramatically impacts our life. Without Jesus, we will know a constant longing for something we don't possess, and we soon learn that nothing in this world can make the longing go away. The good news is that God extends an invitation for us to be in relationship with Him. And Jesus can fill the void. Because of Christ's death and resurrection, we have the opportunity to be reconciled to the Father. "But as many received Him, to them He gave the right to become children of God, to those who believe in His name" (John 1:12).

> *Lord, quench my thirst with living water and fill me with the bread of life. Jesus, I praise You because You are the answer to my greatest longings.*

61

Hear this, all peoples;
give ear, all inhabitants
of the world,
both low and high,
rich and poor together.
My mouth shall
speak wisdom,
and the meditation
of my heart shall give
understanding.

PSALM 49:1–3

In most cultures there are marked distinctions between the rich and poor. Yet God distinguishes people not by financial brackets but by faithfulness. God's Word makes it clear that He imparts wisdom to His people and increases our understanding of His Word and His ways (Psalm 49:3). His blessings are not dictated by our financial status or standing in the community; He distributes His blessing to "both low and high, rich and poor together" (v. 2). Certainly, the Scriptures instruct us to be good stewards of our financial resources. But our finances have no impact on our eternal destiny. The death rate is 100 percent for both the rich and the poor, and we don't get to take our wealth with us when we go: "For when he dies he shall carry nothing away; His glory shall not descend after him" (v. 17). The challenge for all people is to keep our financial status, whatever it may be, in proper perspective. In eternity it will have mattered very little.

Father, I pray I will have proper perspective about my finances. Help me to be a good steward while at the same time focusing on the things that matter most to You.

62

He who loves pleasure
will be a poor man;
he who loves wine and
oil will not be rich.

PROVERBS 21:17

Who doesn't enjoy having a good time? Big events, pleasurable hobbies, and fun trips are blessings to look forward to and part of what makes life memorable. God designed the world with lots of things for us to enjoy. But the pursuit of constant pleasure as an everyday way of life will cause more harm than good. Proverbs 21:17 teaches that those who constantly seek pleasure will become poor. Fun times shouldn't be the primary source of our joy. If we are living in a way that brings glory to God, joy will be a by-product of our everyday life. But if we pursue joy through constant pleasure, we will wind up broke and spiritually empty. The Bible doesn't condemn pleasure or fun times. But if we love pleasure so much that we seek it continually, we are in spiritual danger of looking for fun experiences, rather than God, to fill us.

Father, thank You for creating a world with plenty of things to enjoy. Teach me to keep my pursuit of pleasure in proper balance and to seek You for fulfillment.

63

I rejoice in following
your statutes
as one rejoices in great riches.

PSALM 119:14 NIV

The more time we spend studying God's Word, the more we will love the Scriptures. Psalm 119 celebrates the gift of God's Word as the perfect guide for life. For Christians, the Bible is the handbook for living and is the ultimate guiding authority in the way we live. In his letter to his young protégé, Timothy, the apostle Paul wrote, "All Scripture is God-breathed and is useful for teaching, rebuking, correcting, and training in righteousness" (2 Timothy 3:16 NIV). The term *God-breathed* means the Scriptures are God's Word to humankind. God empowered ordinary men through the power of the Holy Spirit to write the sixty-six books in the biblical canon so we would have the opportunity to know Him, understand His ways, and learn His statutes. There is nothing more valuable than knowing God. As we obey His Word, we will experience joy.

Father, give me a supreme love for Your Word. Help me to understand Your Scriptures so that I will obey Your statutes and rejoice in You.

64

Length of days is in
[wisdom's] right hand,
in her left hand
riches and honor.

PROVERBS 3:16

*C*urrently, the average life expectancy for an American citizen is 78.7 years.[15] Most of us know people who have lived far longer and others who've lived fewer years. Wisdom doesn't guarantee a long life, but as a general rule, those who live wisely cultivate a lifestyle that makes longevity possible. In the book of Proverbs, wisdom is personified as a woman bearing gifts in her hands. In her right hand she holds long life, and in her left riches and honor (3:16). In the same way that wisdom cultivates a lifestyle conducive to a long life, wise living also lends itself to obtaining riches and honor. Wisdom helps us to make good choices on a regular basis. It is a gift from God and is something we should always pursue in greater measure. We grow in wisdom by studying God's Word, paying close attention to His commands, and asking Him to increase our wisdom (James 1:5).

Father, I pray You will continually increase my wisdom. Help me to make wise choices on a daily basis, and teach me to seek Your Word for guidance as I grow in wisdom.

65

By means of their suffering,
he rescues those who suffer.
For he gets their attention
through adversity.

JOB 36:15 NLT

More than a decade ago, the United States experienced a financial crisis that resulted in a stock market crash. From 2007 to 2009, the fallout destroyed $16.4 trillion of American households' net worth, and it wiped out $2 trillion of retirement savings.[16] Countless people lost their entire savings overnight and were financially unprepared for the future. Tragically, it's estimated that more than ten thousand people committed suicide as a result of the financial crisis.[17] But in the face of disaster, many looked to God. Riches don't exempt us from suffering, and sometimes they even cause adversity. But God is faithful in all circumstances. The book of Job says, "By means of their suffering, he rescues those who suffer. For he gets their attention through adversity" (36:15 NLT). In times of suffering, Christians are to look to God for rescue. It doesn't matter if our adversity is financial, physical, mental, or emotional. "God is our refuge and strength, always ready to help in times of trouble" (Psalm 46:1 NLT).

Father, in times of suffering I will be quick to turn to You. Help me to remember that You are my source of constant stability, and You will provide everything I need.

66

Lazy hands make for poverty
but diligent hands
bring wealth.

PROVERBS 10:4 NIV

iligent workers often earn the respect of their peers, but laziness is admired by no one. All of us have dreams and desires that won't happen unless we do the hard work it takes to make those dreams come true. If we want to achieve, we must be willing to make an effort. The Bible is blunt about the topic of laziness: "Lazy hands make for poverty" (Proverbs 10:4 NIV). If we aren't willing to work hard, there is no reason to feel optimistic about attaining financial stability or anything else. But if we habitually put the effort into our endeavors, we have good reason to feel confident about our financial future: "Diligent hands bring wealth" (v. 4 NIV). If you've lacked a good work ethic in the past, there's no reason you have to continue on the same path. Hard work and diligence come from making a decision to do the work for as long as it takes to meet your goals.

> *Lord, I know it is important to work hard every day and always give my best effort. I have no desire to be lazy, and I ask You to help me cultivate an excellent work ethic.*

67

"If you sinful people know how to give good gifts to your children, how much more will your heavenly Father give good gifts to those who ask him."

MATTHEW 7:11 NLT

God intends for prayer to be a focal point in the life of the believer. In the mystery of God's will, He has ordained for believers to move His hand through prayer. Jesus instructed His followers to persistently petition God for our wants and needs: "Keep on asking, and you will receive what you ask for. Keep on seeking, and you will find. Keep on knocking, and the door will be opened" (Matthew 7:7 NLT). Jesus made the point that if we who are sinful know how to give good gifts to our children, we can trust our perfect heavenly Father to do what is best for us when we engage in prayer (v. 11). God invites us to approach Him in prayer. As believers, we have the extraordinary privilege of approaching the God of the universe and asking Him to provide the things we need. As we petition Him in prayer, we can be confident that He will provide what is best.

> *Father, help me to devote myself to prayer. Teach me to trust You as my provider as I make prayer a part of my daily life and grow in my relationship with You.*

68

Wealth is worthless in
the day of wrath,
but righteousness
delivers from death.

PROVERBS 11:4 NIV

od's wrath is not a popular subject, but it's a reality that the Bible repeatedly addresses. The apostle Paul wrote, "For all have sinned and fall short of the glory of God" (Romans 3:23 NIV). Our sin nature has separated us from God, and apart from Christ, we will face the wrath of God for our sins. But the gospel teaches that Christ died on our behalf, and because of Jesus' atonement for our sins, we can be reconciled to the Father (Romans 5:8). Apart from Christ, we have no righteousness in our own merit. But "God made him who had no sin to be sin for us, so that in him we might become the righteousness of God" (2 Corinthians 5:21 NIV). Billions of dollars will be of no help if faced with wrath, but Christ's righteousness delivers us from the wrath of God, and by it we inherit eternal life (Proverbs 11:4).

> *Jesus, I praise You for Your sacrifice on the cross that atoned for the sins of humanity. Thank You for being my Savior and removing the wrath of God from me and replacing it with eternal life.*

69

The LORD is my shepherd;
I shall not want.

PSALM 23:1

In Psalm 23, King David made a declaration of his confidence in the Lord's provision. Not surprisingly, David used a metaphor of a shepherd and his sheep. In David's era, shepherding was a common profession and one with which most people were familiar. Sheep are notorious for wandering off from the flock and being chronically vulnerable. A flock of sheep is entirely dependent on the goodness of the shepherd because without the shepherd's care they would quickly perish. A good shepherd provides food, water, and protection from predators. David wrote, "The LORD is my shepherd; I shall not want" (Psalm 23:1). In the same way that sheep are prone to wander from the flock, God's people tend to drift. But Jesus faithfully tends to us like a loving shepherd and provides everything we need to thrive. Apart from Christ's constant care and provision, we too are vulnerable from outside threats that can destroy us. But if the Lord is our shepherd, then like David, we will find we have everything we need to flourish.

Jesus, thank You for being the Good Shepherd. Thank You for providing everything I need to live a life that is pleasing to You.

70

God will generously provide
all you need. Then you will
always have everything
you need and plenty left
over to share with others.

2 CORINTHIANS 9:8 NLT

When the apostle Paul wrote his second letter to the Corinthians, he addressed the topic of generosity: "For God loves a person who gives cheerfully" (2 Corinthians 9:7 NLT). We don't honor God when we give begrudgingly or with strings attached. Yet when we give cheerfully, it demonstrates a heart that is content in God's ability to provide and expresses a willingness to share His blessings. People who are generous can be trusted with even more of God's blessings because they don't tend to be greedy or horde what they've been given. Paul encouraged the church at Corinth that God would provide for their needs and that they would have plenty left over to share with others (v. 8). Generosity, or lack of it, is a matter of faith. When we are confident that God will provide, we can cheerfully give knowing that He will replenish our resources and continue to provide in a way that allows for habitual generosity.

> Father, I pray for faith that makes me a cheerful giver. Help me to be mindful that it is more blessed to give than to receive. Thank You for the generosity You continually show me.

71

A good name is to be chosen
rather than great riches,
loving favor rather
than silver and gold.

PROVERBS 22:1

*E*very day, whether we realize it or not, we are making a reputation for ourselves. Our behavior, habits, attitude, character, and work ethic speak volumes to those around us, and people form opinions based on what they see. Our reputations are formed from these opinions. The Bible teaches that a "good name" or a good reputation is more valuable than wealth and riches and to be more highly sought after than silver or gold (Proverbs 22:1); the point being that our character is more significant than wealth. Most of us spend a good deal of time thinking about our budgets and money. How much time do you spend assessing your character? When is the last time you sought to improve on a character flaw? A good reputation can't be bought; it can only be earned. A good name gives us favor and influence with other people and opens up the door for quality relationships, which is something we all long for and hope to enjoy.

> *Father, since my reputation will reflect my character, please help me address my character flaws and seek integrity.*

72

Good will come to those who
are generous and lend freely,
who conduct their
affairs with justice.

PSALM 112:5 NIV

enerosity is the cure for many of the problems created by wealth. Greed is a perpetual threat to all people, but those who are wealthy are at risk of exploiting others in an effort to accumulate more wealth. Intentional generosity is the remedy for greed. When we experience the joy of giving, there will be less temptation to cling as tightly to what we possess. Generosity begins with a decision that ultimately becomes a lifestyle. The fear of losing wealth can be a snare for those who have become accustomed to being comfortable. Generosity shows that our faith is in God rather than our bank accounts. Generous people benefit just as much from generosity as their recipients do. In today's scripture, the psalmist wrote that "good will come to those who are generous" (Psalm 112:5 NIV). Generosity keeps us from becoming enslaved by our resources.

Father, generosity is good for all of us. Please give me a generous spirit so that I will experience joy each time I give. Guard my heart against greed, and teach me to be an extravagant giver.

73

As for the rich in this present age, charge them not to be haughty, nor to set their hopes on the uncertainty of riches, but on God, who richly provides us with everything to enjoy.

1 TIMOTHY 6:17 ESV

For modern-day believers, just as in the New Testament times, possessing wealth is neither a sin nor a sign of God's blessing. Many godly people are poor, and some wicked people are rich. But wealthy people have to take care to guard against temptations that are often associated with riches. The apostle Paul instructed the rich not to be haughty or conceited. Rich people will be faced with the temptation to put on an air of superiority, and Paul, in 1 Timothy 6:17, urged the wealthy to avoid that trap. For the wealthy, there is also a greater temptation to place their hope on their finances rather than on God. Paul taught the rich and poor alike to set their hope on God alone because He provides security that no amount of riches can provide. Earthly riches can fail us, but God's wealth and security are limitless: "For every beast of the forest is mine, the cattle on a thousand hills" (Psalm 50:10 ESV).

Father, help me to guard against arrogance and conceit. I pray my trust and confidence will be based solely on Your provision and that if my wealth increases I will not set my heart on it.

74

Do not wear yourself
out to get rich;
do not trust your
own cleverness.
Cast but a glance at riches,
and they are gone,
for they will surely
sprout wings
and fly off to the sky
like an eagle.

PROVERBS 23:4–5 NIV

*I*t's possible to destroy our health trying to get rich and then spend every dime we possess trying to restore our health. The Bible instructs all believers to have an excellent work ethic, but we also need the wisdom to know when to rest. For this reason, God provided a Sabbath day and warned about the perils of exhaustion in the pursuit of wealth: "Do not wear yourself out to get rich" (Psalm 23:4 NIV). Perhaps you've heard someone say, "No one on their deathbed wishes they had spent more time at the office." At the end of our lives, we will want to have invested in the things that matter most. Financial stewardship and working hard are important, but we need wisdom to strike a good balance between work and rest.

> *Father, it is important to have the wisdom to know when to work and when to rest. Help me to prioritize my time in light of what matters most, and teach me to spend my days in ways that bring glory to You.*

75

The sleep of a laboring
man is sweet,
whether he eats
little or much;
but the abundance of the rich
will not permit him to sleep.

ECCLESIASTES 5:12

Nothing compares to putting in a full day's work and crawling in bed at night knowing you gave your best effort. Sleep usually comes quickly to those who work hard all day. King Solomon wrote, "The sleep of a laboring man is sweet" (Ecclesiastes 5:12). In the garden of Eden, before the fall of man, work was a good thing. But after the fall, work was impacted by sin (Genesis 3:17). It was then that work became difficult. But God's design for work is still good, and without it, humankind is not operating in the way God designed us. Our work schedules dramatically impact our sleep. Those who don't engage in work are less likely to get fatigued during the day, and as a result they sleep poorly: "But the abundance of the rich will not permit him to sleep" (Ecclesiastes 5:12). Work is intended for our good, and putting in a full day will promote sleep on a regular basis.

Father, thank You for my work. I pray I will be motivated to work so hard in the day that I sleep soundly every night. Help me always to give my best effort.

76

Let not the wise boast
of their wisdom
or the strong boast
of their strength
or the rich boast
of their riches.

JEREMIAH 9:23 NIV

*M*odern-day society is far from humble. In a selfie-driven culture, it's commonplace for people to draw attention to themselves. Prior generations were more humble about their accomplishments, and it was considered poor taste to brag. But social media provides whoever desires a platform an opportunity to make a name for themselves. But the prophet Jeremiah cautioned, "Let not the wise boast in their wisdom or the strong boast of their strength or the rich boast of their riches" (Jeremiah 9:23 NIV). God's people are not to boast about anything but the Lord. We are not to call attention to our intelligence, social status, or possessions. If we want to boast, God says to "boast about this: that they have the understanding to know me, that I am the LORD, who exercises kindness, justice and righteousness on earth, for in these I delight" (v. 24 NIV).

> *Lord, I will not boast about anything but You. When I get out of line, convict me quickly so that I will be humble, as Your Word instructs.*

77

The wicked in his pride
persecutes the poor;
let them be caught in
the plots which they
have devised.

PSALM 10:2

*P*ride is a dangerous sin and often motivates the biggest mistakes we make. It doesn't discriminate, impacting people from every race, gender, culture, and socioeconomic group. It clouds our thinking and gives us a false sense of entitlement and superiority. Prideful people believe the world owes them something. Pride warps our expectations and deceives us into believing our actions are acceptable when they aren't. Everyone needs to guard against being too proud, but those who are in positions of power or who possess wealth must be the most vigilant about it. The psalmist pointed out that pride prompts the wicked to persecute the poor (Psalm 10:2). Sadly, pride can make us treat people poorly. If we are wise, we will continually keep our pride in check and go to any length to rid ourselves of its impact on our character.

Father, I need Your help in guarding against pride. Teach me to humble myself and to walk in humility before You and others.

78

A faithful person will
be richly blessed,
but one eager to get rich
will not go unpunished.

PROVERBS 28:20 NIV

$\mathcal{S}$ etting goals and taking steps toward financial stability are wise pursuits, but the desire to get rich quickly will end up in disaster. Solomon was among the wealthiest men who ever lived, and he penned much of the book of Proverbs. Not surprisingly, Proverbs has plenty to say about pursuing and managing wealth. God's Word instructs us that faithfulness is the pathway to being richly blessed. People who yearn to get rich quickly often succumb to dishonest methods that are not pleasing to God. Managing our day-to-day life with integrity and devoting ourselves to habitually doing the right thing invite God's blessing. But devious schemes that promise a quick payoff will be punished. Acquiring wealth is not a sinful endeavor if it's pursued with godly character and good intentions. Maintaining integrity as we pursue our goals is even more important than achieving them.

Father, please help me develop godly integrity. Increase my faithfulness and make me trustworthy as You guard my heart against dishonest gain.

79

Like a partridge that
hatches eggs it did not lay
are those who gain riches
by unjust means.
When their lives are half gone,
their riches will desert them,
and in the end they will
prove to be fools.

JEREMIAH 17:11 NIV

eadline news has reported high-profile Ponzi schemes that lure unsuspecting investors with early payoffs that build trust and encourage greater risks. Later, when innocent investors risk greater sums of money, they are swindled and end up losing everything to thieves. The Bible compares these and other types of fraudulent scammers to a bird who hatches an egg it didn't lay, and it predicts a dreadful future for those who engage in crooked tactics: "Their riches will desert them, and in the end they will prove to be fools" (Jeremiah 17:11 NIV). Fraudulent money schemes always have a mastermind who devises the wicked plan. A great deal of thought and effort go into engineering these scams, and for a time the criminals might consider themselves clever. But in the end they will lose their wealth and will be thought of as fools.

> *Father, I pray for wisdom and discernment as I save and invest money. Guard my heart so that I will not be led astray from Your path.*

80

By humility and the
fear of the LORD
are riches and honor and life.

PROVERBS 22:4

*S*elf-absorption is a trap that ends in misery. The more we focus on ourselves, the smaller our world becomes. The prescription for self-centeredness is humility. But that doesn't mean we have a poor opinion of ourselves. It simply means we think of ourselves less and we don't consider our needs and desires as the most important thing. The Bible identifies humility and the fear of the Lord as attributes that lead to riches, honor, and life (Proverbs 22:4). To fear the Lord means to honor and revere Him above all things. Fearing the Lord helps us keep a humble attitude because reverence for God exalts Him as the most important thing in life and rightfully places us in submission to Him. Ironically, focusing on our own needs doesn't lead to fulfillment. A lifestyle of humility and fear of the Lord leads us to discover the best things this life has to offer.

> *Father, please help me to develop a humble attitude in which I revere You above all things. Guard me against self-absorption so that I live with an outward-focused mind-set.*

81

"No one can serve two masters. For you will hate one and love the other; you will be devoted to one and despise the other. You cannot serve God and be enslaved to money."

MATTHEW 6:24 NLT

A divided heart is in constant conflict. In Jesus' Sermon on the Mount, He didn't mince words when speaking about God and money. Jesus said, "You cannot serve God and be enslaved to money" (Matthew 6:24 NLT). To follow Jesus, we must love Him more than we love anything else (10:37). If we are enslaved to money, our hearts aren't capable of being ruled by the love of Christ. Interestingly, in our pursuit of wealth, it is Jesus we are looking for. People who are ruled by money are looking for peace, security, and fulfillment like everyone else. But idols never deliver what they promise, and being ruled by money will cause us to come up empty. Jesus said, "Seek the Kingdom of God above all else, and live righteously, and he will give you everything you need" (6:33 NLT).

> *Jesus, I want to serve You and not money. Give me both the wisdom to see that You are the answer to all my needs and a heart that seeks You above all things.*

82

Each of you must bring
a gift in proportion to
the way the LORD your
God has blessed you.

DEUTERONOMY 16:17 NIV

In both the Old and New Testaments, God instructs His people to give in proportion to the measure in which He has given (Deuteronomy 16:17; 2 Corinthians 8:12). For some, there might be a temptation to avoid giving or to give the bare minimum. For New Testament believers living on this side of the cross, withholding our tithes or giving the bare minimum aren't worthy options. When we are mindful that Jesus gave everything He had on our behalf, how can we respond by giving nothing or even giving the minimum? Jesus didn't give the minimum for us. He gave His life. Christians are the recipients of the most extravagant gift ever given, and to respond as misers demonstrates a lack of gratitude and a low supply of faith. The only appropriate response is for Christ followers to be the most generous people on the planet.

Lord, thank You for the ultimate sacrifice You willingly paid on the cross. In response, I pray I will be extravagantly generous with my resources and constantly filled with gratitude.

83

Honor the LORD with
your possessions,
and with the firstfruits
of all your increase;
so your barns will be
filled with plenty,
and your vats will overflow
with new wine.

PROVERBS 3:9–10

On Sundays it's common for people to drop a couple of spare dollars in the collection plate at church. If you aren't in the habit of giving, that might be a good place to start, but the ultimate goal is to give from your "firstfruits," which means that the first money you delegate from your income goes to giving. Honoring God above everything else means we are obedient to the tithe before we spend in other areas. Some people are in the habit of giving God what's left over, but as we can see from today's scripture, that's not what God's Word calls us to do. When we are obedient to God with our money, we can be confident that He will provide everything we need.

> *Father, I pray that my checkbook will demonstrate that You are Lord of my life. Please increase my joy in giving, and help me to obey and trust You as I give.*

84

For you know the grace of our Lord Jesus Christ, that though he was rich, yet for your sake he became poor, so that you by his poverty might become rich.

2 CORINTHIANS 8:9 ESV

*I*f we aren't mindful of the cost, it's easy to ignore the sacrifice it took for Jesus to come to earth in the flesh. The apostle Paul wrote to the church at Philippi, "Have this mind among yourselves, which is yours in Christ Jesus, who, though he was in the form of God, did not count equality with God a thing to be grasped, but emptied himself, by taking the form of a servant, being born in the likeness of men" (Philippians 2:5–7 ESV). Jesus set aside the vast resources that come with His lordship to take on flesh and become poor at our expense. Jesus modeled the reality that people are more important than position. As Christ followers, there are times when we too are called to make sacrifices for other people. When we do, we shouldn't view our sacrifices as a burden but rather an opportunity to live in the way Jesus intends for us.

> *Jesus, I am awestruck by the fact that You became poor so You could serve humankind. Help me to model Your sacrificial giving and live in a way that honors You.*

85

"So don't worry about these things, saying, 'What will we eat? What will we drink? What will we wear?' These things dominate the thoughts of unbelievers, but your heavenly Father already knows all your needs. Seek the Kingdom of God above all else, and live righteously, and he will give you everything you need."

MATTHEW 6:31–33 NLT

*H*olocaust survivor Corrie Ten Boom said, "Worry does not empty tomorrow of its sorrow, it empties today of strength."[18] Worry is a universal problem that Jesus instructed His people to avoid. At its core, worrying about finances reveals a lack of faith that God will provide everything we need. Jesus said that worrying about food and clothing dominates the thoughts of unbelievers, but it shouldn't be a trait of those who profess Him as Lord. Our heavenly Father is intimately aware of what's going on in the lives of His children. The number of hairs on our head doesn't change without His knowledge (Matthew 10:30), so we can be confident that He knows our exact needs and is willing to provide. When we are convinced that God is good, He is able, and He loves us, there is no reason for us to worry about lack. We can trust that our Father will provide.

> *Father, thank You for being intimately aware of my needs. Help me to trust You and not to worry, because You will provide everything I need.*

86

Whoever puts up security for
a stranger will surely suffer,
but whoever refuses to shake
hands in pledge is safe.

PROVERBS 11:15 NIV

It's not uncommon for people who have money in savings or a good credit standing to be asked for loans from family or friends. To "put up security" means to cosign a loan on someone else's behalf. The writer of Proverbs points out that cosigning for a stranger will cause suffering (11:15). Most people wouldn't consider cosigning a loan for a stranger, but what about when a friend or family member is in need? For the most part, making decisions about loaning money and extending financial favors are case-by-case decisions, and sometimes it's hard to know the right thing to do. It's possible to lend with good intentions and have things turn out poorly. Countless relationships have ended over unpaid loans. Choosing to loan money or to cosign a loan always comes with a degree of risk that is both financial and relational, so these decisions call for wisdom and prayer.

Father, I pray You will give me wisdom to manage my finances and the insight I need when it's hard to know the right thing to do.

87

My God will use his wonderful
riches in Christ Jesus to give
you everything you need.

PHILIPPIANS 4:19 NCV

When Paul was in prison, he wrote to the church at Philippi, and near the end of his letter he thanked them for their financial support (Philippians 4:10–11). Using language from the Old Testament, he compared their gift to a fragrant aroma and said it was pleasing to the Lord (v. 19; Genesis 8:20–21). Paul viewed their financial contribution as a sacrificial act of worship to God.[19] Paul knew that God would provide the Philippians with spiritual blessings as well as supply their physical needs. The Philippians had provided sacrificially for a brother in Christ in need, and God would see to it that they were cared for as well. This reality holds true for modern-day believers. God provides for us so we can provide for others.

Father, thank You for Your generosity. Help me to be quick to open my hand to those in need so that I will experience joy in giving. Teach me to trust Your provision, and increase my desire to give.

88

When God gives someone
wealth and possessions,
and the ability to enjoy
them, to accept their lot
and be happy in their toil—
this is a gift of God.

ECCLESIASTES 5:19 NIV

*H*ave you ever known a wealthy person who lacked the ability to enjoy his or her work, wealth, or possessions? It's a perplexing thing to see someone who possesses everything a person could want or need without the capability of enjoying those blessings. King Solomon was filled with God-given wisdom, and when he wrote the book of Ecclesiastes, he revealed that God gives people the ability to enjoy what we have. Regardless of our income, if we have the ability to enjoy our lot in life and be happy with our work, it is a gift from God (5:19). If we find ourselves in a season of life when we aren't enjoying our work and circumstances as much as we'd like, it's wise to pray and ask God to give us the ability to enjoy our day-to-day routine. At times, our lack of enjoyment is more about our attitude than our circumstances. Our attitudes can be adjusted even when our circumstances cannot.

Father, You give me the ability to enjoy my day-to-day responsibilities. Help me truly to look forward to my daily work and to enjoy and appreciate what I have.

89

Two things I request
of You . . .
Give me neither poverty
nor riches—
feed me with the food
allotted to me;
lest I be full and deny You,
and say, "Who is the LORD?"
or lest I be poor and steal,
and profane the
name of my God.

PROVERBS 30:7–9

$\mathcal{P}$overty and riches both come with spiritual liabilities. Agur, the writer of Proverbs 30, was so concerned with the risks that he prayed, "Give me neither poverty nor riches" (v. 8). Distinct temptations accompany both poverty and wealth, and it's wise to be mindful of both. If we have an excess of wealth, there is a temptation to wrongly believe we don't need God because we trust in our financial resources to meet our needs. For those suffering extreme poverty, there is a temptation to take matters into our own hands and steal. Both extremes dishonor God. Agur prayed for a middle-class lifestyle, but people in every tax bracket must be mindful of the risks of drifting from God.

Father, no matter what my finances reflect, I pray I will value You above all things. Teach me to live a life that honors Your name and reflects Your glory.

90

Those who desire to be rich fall into temptation, into a snare, into many senseless and harmful desires that plunge people into ruin and destruction.

1 TIMOTHY 6:9 ESV

When the apostle Paul wrote 1 Timothy, he wrote with the desire to equip his young protégé for ministry. Paul didn't condemn material possessions, but he did warn against the desire to be rich and having a love of money, which he identified as the root of all kinds of evil (1 Timothy 6:10). The correlation between desiring to be rich and false teaching had been a chronic problem in the church, and Paul cautioned Timothy to avoid that pitfall. Instead, Paul encouraged Timothy to pursue other things: "But as for you, O man of God, flee these things. Pursue righteousness, godliness, faith, love, steadfastness, gentleness" (v. 11 ESV). Paul understood that authentic Christian ministry could never be motivated by greed, only by a love for Christ and accountability to Him.

> *Jesus, guard my heart from anything that could impact my devotion to You. Teach me to walk in Your ways as I pursue righteousness, godliness, faith, love, steadfastness, and gentleness.*

91

The sun rises with burning heat and dries up the plants. The flower falls off, and its beauty is gone. In the same way the rich will die while they are still taking care of business.

JAMES 1:11 NCV

When we're young, it's hard to imagine ever growing old or dying. But as we age, we bury loved ones too soon and realize that our time in this world won't last forever. To complicate matters, none of us know how much time we have. The Bible makes it clear that the poor and rich are alike in death. Wealth is temporary and provides no advantage to us before God. In James 1:11, Jesus' brother, the apostle James, compared the rich to a flower that dies in the sun. Both poverty and riches provide enormous temptation to focus on the things of the world rather than our relationship with God. But we must be mindful that our time here will come to an end, and the only thing left to take into eternity will be our relationship with God.

> *Father, what a beautiful gift today is. I want to use my time wisely and invest in my relationship with You. Help me live with an awareness that my time on earth is short but my soul is eternal.*

92

A generous man devises
generous things,
and by generosity
he shall stand.

ISAIAH 32:8

One person can make an enormous impact on the world. We're all aware of well-known people who used their lives to bring a great deal of good to the world as well as some who caused a harrowing amount of evil. We have a choice about how we live. The prophet Isaiah wrote about a kingdom of human nobility that was made possible by the grace of God: "A generous man devises generous things, and by generosity he shall stand" (Isaiah 32:8). People who are able should aim to bring good to other people and by doing so advance the kingdom of God on earth. In terms of kindness, generosity, and compassion, how would you like to be remembered? Will the people in your sphere of influence be better off because of you? God has given all of us the ability to impact our world for the better, and there is an expectation that we will. Jesus said, "Let your light so shine before men, that they may see your good works and glorify your Father in heaven" (Matthew 5:16).

Father, please send me opportunities to make this world better and to be good to every person You put in my path. I want to advance Your kingdom on earth with my life.

93

So I thought I should ask
these brothers to go to you
before we do. They will
finish getting in order the
generous gift you promised
so it will be ready when
we come. And it will be a
generous gift—not one that
you did not want to give.

2 CORINTHIANS 9:5 NCV

When Paul wrote 2 Corinthians, he addressed the topic of a previously promised gift that the Corinthians had committed to giving. Paul sent Titus along with two other unnamed people to travel to Corinth before his arrival to make sure it was ready when Paul arrived. Paul didn't want the Corinthians to give begrudgingly or without a sense of joy. He wrote, "And it will be a generous gift—not one that you did not want to give" (2 Corinthians 9:5 NCV). A willing attitude and cheerful spirit characterize true giving. Giving a gift against our will does not honor God, nor does it show goodwill to the recipient. Giving is a matter of faith. If we can't give with a willing attitude, we need to rethink our gift and determine why we are feeling reluctant. True giving comes from the heart and is motivated by our love for God and other people.

Father, when I give, I will give with a willing attitude. Please increase my love for You and other people so that giving will come naturally to me.

94

You open Your hand
and satisfy the desire
of every living thing.

PSALM 145:16

*I*n every sense, God is our provider. He provides for all people, animals, plants, and every living thing. King David wrote, "The eyes of all look expectantly to You, and You give their food in due season" (Psalm 145:15). If we take the time to consider how God designed the food chain and the way He feeds wildlife, we will marvel at His ways. Every beast in the field and bird in the air is sustained by God's provision. The same is true for all people. The apostle Paul said, "He gives to all life, breath, and all things" (Acts 17:25). God doesn't just provide us with the things we need. He also provides many of our wants and desires: "You open Your hand and satisfy the desire of every living thing" (Psalm 145:16). Recognizing that God is our provider shifts stress off of our shoulders. When we recognize His goodness and know He is in control, we can relax and trust His faithfulness.

> *Father, thank You for being the ultimate provider. Help me to live with an awareness that You are in control of all things so that I will constantly bear witness to Your power and glory.*

95

The righteous eats to the
satisfying of his soul,
but the stomach of the
wicked shall be in want.

PROVERBS 13:25

I f we view God as tightfisted and reluctant to provide, we have a false view of God that we have picked up from someplace other than Scripture. The Bible reveals that God has a long history of not only providing for the basic needs of the righteous, but providing abundantly. "The righteous eats to the satisfying of his soul, but the stomach of the wicked shall be in want" (Proverbs 13:25). At times, the wicked find themselves in want due to sin and poor decisions, but God is faithful to provide for His people. God is never stingy; in fact, the Bible constantly bears witness to His generosity. God provides for us physically, emotionally, and spiritually. The apostle Paul wrote, "Now to Him who is able to do exceedingly abundantly above all that we ask or think, according to the power that works in us, to Him be glory" (Ephesians 3:20–21). God doesn't just provide barely enough for us; He satisfies our souls (Proverbs 13:25).

Father, thank You for Your extravagant provision. All praise to You for Your kindness and generosity. I pray my thoughts of You will be accurate and biblical and that I will know You as You truly are.

96

Why do you spend money
for what is not bread,
and your wages for what
does not satisfy?
Listen carefully to Me,
and eat what is good,
and let your soul delight
itself in abundance.

ISAIAH 55:2

*A*s people living in a fallen world, there are times when we feel a deep longing in our souls. Perhaps it's an emptiness that needs filling or a heartache that needs tending to. In the West, we live in a prosperous culture, and it's common for us to respond to those yearnings and feelings of emptiness with things that can distract us. We might shop too much, lose ourselves in our work, distract ourselves online, or engage in destructive habits that might offer temporary relief but cannot satisfy. The prophet Isiah wrote, "Why do you spend money for what is not bread, and your wages for what does not satisfy? Listen carefully to Me, and eat what is good, and let your soul delight itself in abundance" (Isaiah 55:2). What we are really looking for is Jesus. The longings we experience are meant to be filled by Him.

> *Jesus, when I am feeling empty, I will look to You. Teach me to avoid looking to idols to do for me what only You can do. Let my longings drive me to You.*

97

He who tills his land will
be satisfied with bread,
but he who follows frivolity
is devoid of understanding.

PROVERBS 12:11

It's likely that a high percentage of full-time employees have spent time daydreaming of what life might be like without being strapped to a forty-hour-a-week job. Although many of us like to think about what we might do with ample free time, the Bible cautions us not to abandon our work for unwise pursuits: "He who tills his land will be satisfied with bread, but he who follows frivolity is devoid of understanding" (Proverbs 12:11). At times, going to work day in and day out seems like an endless cycle that repeats itself with no visible gain. Sometimes we feel as though we're just caught up in the daily grind. But daily effort produces remarkable results. Progress isn't made by things we do occasionally but by things we do consistently. Our work lives are important, and our employment is the primary way God provides for our finances: "If anyone will not work, neither shall he eat" (2 Thessalonians 3:10).

> *Father, please give me a correct perspective of work. Provide me with good work to do, and help me to do it to the best of my abilities.*

98

Whoever loves money
never has enough;
whoever loves wealth is never
satisfied with their income.
This too is meaningless.

ECCLESIASTES 5:10 NIV

*L*earning to be content will dramatically increase our happiness. Greed is a destructive force that has the potential to ruin our lives because it insists there is never enough. Greed creates a perpetual attitude of dissatisfaction and an inability to enjoy the present. Solomon wrote in today's scripture that "whoever loves money never has enough" (Ecclesiastes 5:10). The love of money will keep us stuck like hamsters in a wheel, always in pursuit of the next thing. Solomon said that makes for a meaningless life. Contentment will never be found in a higher salary, a new purchase, or a heftier savings account. While there's nothing wrong with pursuing goals, the love of money will rob us of present satisfaction. If we can't be happy with what we have, we will never be satisfied with what we attain. Satisfaction doesn't come from a status we achieve. It comes from a relationship with Jesus.

Lord, I pray I will not get caught in the trap of dissatisfaction and that I will be content in every situation. Teach me to set godly goals without getting caught up in the love of money.

99

"Whoever can be trusted with very little can also be trusted with much, and whoever is dishonest with very little will also be dishonest with much."

LUKE 16:10 NIV

There's a good chance you've heard people say that if they had more money, they would be more generous. The truth is, that's seldom the case. Our faithfulness is determined by our character, not our bank accounts. Church pews are filled with millionaires who give nothing and poor people who give sacrificially. At its core, giving is an issue of spiritual character and integrity and has little to do with how much we possess. Jesus said, "Whoever can be trusted with very little can also be trusted with much, and whoever is dishonest with very little will also be dishonest with much" (Luke 16:10 NIV). Jesus was making the point that people who can be trusted with very little have the character to be trusted with more, while those who are dishonest with a little would continue to be dishonest if given greater amounts. The final factor has nothing to do with how much we possess but rather with our faithfulness and character.

> *Lord, I desire to be someone You can trust with money. Whether I have a little or much, help me to be faithful to honor You with what I have.*

100

The wicked borrows
and does not repay,
but the righteous shows
mercy and gives.

PSALM 37:21

*I*n Psalm 37, King David communicated some of the ways the Lord blesses His people (Psalm 37:21–31). David wrote, "The wicked borrows and does not repay, but the righteous shows mercy and gives" (v. 21). It is incumbent on believers to be upright in their financial dealings, and part of this involves repaying debts. This is especially true when the wicked borrow money with no intention of paying back what they owe, creating hardship for the person they borrowed from. Righteous people, however, are often on the giving side of the equation, sharing from whatever they have, be it much or little. God's Word is to be heeded for more than one reason. First and foremost, as Christians, we are called to live in obedience to His Word. But as we obey, we soon learn that God's ways are wise and beneficial for us.

Father, my heart is to obey You in every circumstance. Teach me to live in a way that is merciful to others as I share what I have with those in need.

Notes

CHAPTER 5

1. ESV Study Bible (Wheaton, IL: Crossway, 2008), note 1911.

CHAPTER 9

2. "Media Advertising Spending in the United States from 2015 to 2021 (in Billion U.S. Dollars)," Statista, https://www.statista.com/statistics/272314/advertising-spending-in-the-us/.

CHAPTER 10

3. John MacArthur, *The MacArthur New Testament Commentary: Matthew 16–23* (Chicago: Moody, 1988), 268–69.

CHAPTER 13

4. Mike Holmes, "What Would Happen if the Church Tithed?," *Relevant*, March 8, 2016, https://relevantmagazine.com/love-and-money/what-would-happen-if-church-tithed.
5. Holmes, "What Would Happen if the Church Tithed?"

CHAPTER 17

6. Gregory Besiger, "This Is How Much Time Employees Spend Slacking Off," *New York Post*, July 29, 2017, https://nypost.com/2017/07/29/this-is-how-much-time-employees-spend-slacking-off/.

CHAPTER 22

7. John MacArthur, *The MacArthur New Testament Commentary: 1 Timothy* (Chicago: Moody Publishers, 1995), 198, 202.

CHAPTER 26

8.   ESV Study Bible, note 955.

CHAPTER 28

9.   Emmie Martin, "Americans Are More Stressed About Money Than Work or Relationships—Here's Why," CNBC, June 26, 2018, https://www.cnbc.com/2018/06/26/money-is-more-stressful-than-work-or-relationships.html.

CHAPTER 33

10.   "Hunger in America," Farmers and Hunters Feeding the Hungry, https://www.fhfh.org/hunger-in-america.html?gclid=EAIaIQobChMInK3SnLHN3gIVko2z Ch3xawsLEAAYAiAAEgKgNPD_BwE.

CHAPTER 41

11.   Warren B. Wiersbe, *Psalms 1–89: Be Worshipful, Glorifying God for Who He Is* (Colorado Springs, CO: David C. Cook, 1982), 93.

CHAPTER 43

12.   John MacArthur, *The MacArthur New Testament Commentary: Luke 18–24* (Chicago: Moody Publishers, 2000), 297.

CHAPTER 45

13.   Wiersbe, *Psalms 1–89*, 150.

CHAPTER 50

14.   ESV Study Bible, note 1159.

CHAPTER 64

15.   Grace Donnelly, "Here's Why Life Expectancy in the U.S. Dropped Again This Year," *Fortune*, February 9, 2018, http://fortune.com/2018/02/09/us-life-expectancy-dropped-again/.

CHAPTER 65

16. Tara Clarke, "2008 Stock Market Crash Causes and Aftermath," Money Morning, June 26, 2015, https://moneymorning.com/2015/06/26/2008-stock-market-crash-causes-and-aftermath/.

17. Melanie Haiken, "More Than 10,000 Suicides Tied to Economic Crisis, Study Says," *Forbes*, June 12, 2014, https://www.forbes.com/sites/melaniehaiken/2014/06/12/more-than-10000-suicides-tied-to-economic-crisis-study-says/#5c8700c77ae2.

CHAPTER 85

18. Corrie Ten Boom, *Clippings from My Notebook* (Nashville: Thomas Nelson, 1982).

CHAPTER 87

19. John MacArthur, *The MacArthur New Testament Commentary: Philippians* (Chicago: Moody, 2001), 307.

My Favorite Bible Verses

....

....

....

....

....

....

....

....

....

....

....

....

....

....

....

....

....